The Boreal
FOREST

A Year in the World's Largest Land Biome

L. E. Carmichael • Josée Bisaillon

Kids Can Press

For Brian, who makes everything possible — L.E.C.

For Margot, who is as amazing as all the animals in this book — J.B.

Acknowledgments

Thank you to the following scientists who reviewed the manuscript: Dr. Jill Johnstone, Research Affiliate, Institute of Arctic Biology, University of Alaska Fairbanks; Dr. Maara Packalen, Research Biologist, Ontario Ministry of Natural Resources and Forestry; Alasdair Veitch, wildlife biologist; Dr. Kara Webster, Research Scientist, Canadian Forest Service. Thanks also to Dr. Greg Wilson, Dr. Chris Kyle and Andrew Chapeskie.

Text © 2020 Lindsey Carmichael
Illustrations © 2020 Josée Bisaillon

Kids Can Press gratefully acknowledges the financial support of the Government of Ontario, through Ontario Creates; the Ontario Arts Council; the Canada Council for the Arts; and the Government of Canada for our publishing activity.

Published in Canada and the U.S. by Kids Can Press Ltd.
25 Dockside Drive, Toronto, ON M5A 0B5

Kids Can Press is a Corus Entertainment Inc. company

www.kidscanpress.com

The artwork in this book was rendered in mixed media.
The text is set in Panforte Pro and VAG Rounded.

Edited by Katie Scott
Designed by Marie Bartholomew

Printed and bound in Malaysia in 10/2019 by Tien Wah Press (Pte) Ltd.

CM 20 0 9 8 7 6 5 4 3 2 1

Library and Archives Canada Cataloguing in Publication

Title: The boreal forest : a year in the world's largest land biome /
written by L. E. Carmichael ; illustrated by Josée Bisaillon.

Names: Carmichael, L. E. (Lindsey E.), author. | Bisaillon, Josée, illustrator.

Description: Includes index.

Identifiers: Canadiana 20190109637 | ISBN 9781525300448 (hardcover)

Subjects: LCSH: Taiga ecology — Juvenile literature. | LCSH: Taigas — Juvenile literature.

Classification: LCC QH541.5.T3 C37 2020 | DDC j578.73/7 — dc23

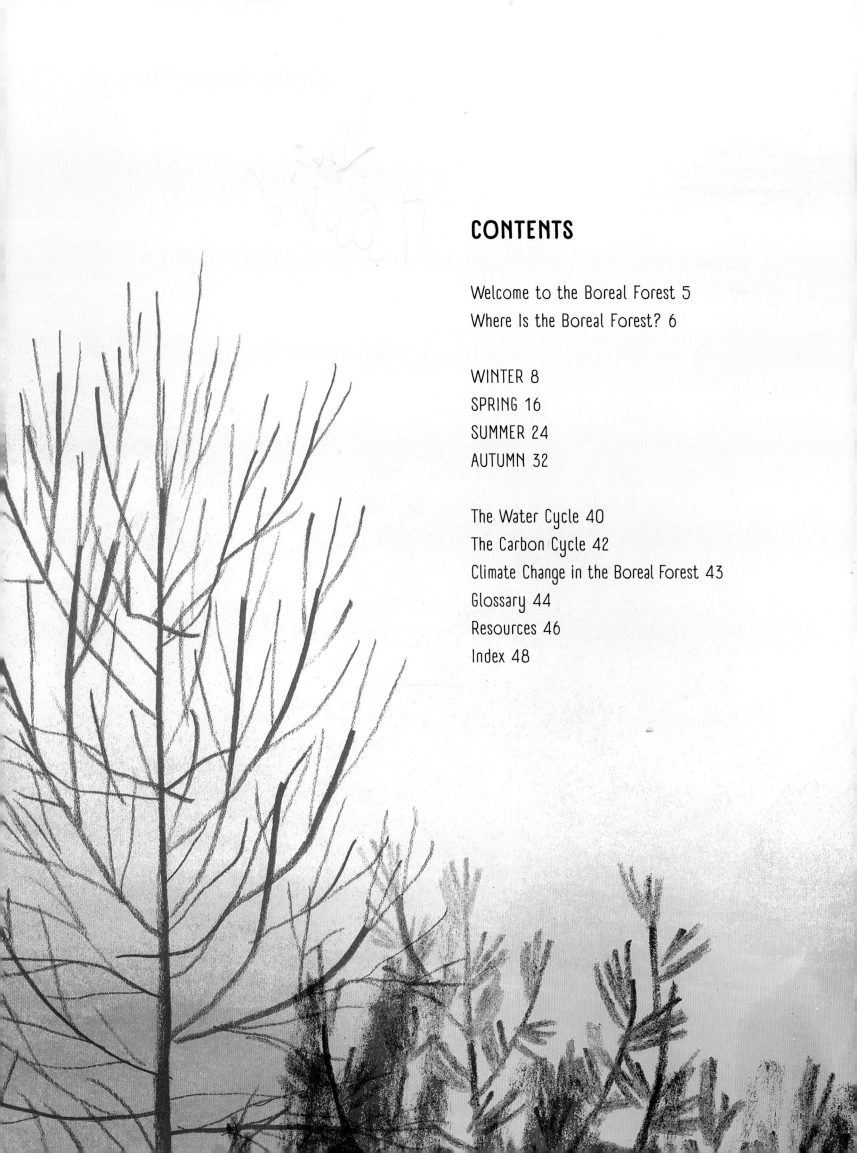

CONTENTS

Glaciers melt, soil breathes,
seeds fly on a warming breeze.
Trees creep ever, ever north.
Centuries pass, climate changes.
A forest is born.

Welcome to the Boreal Forest

The boreal forest is young, less than eight thousand
years old. Before then, during the Ice Age, glaciers covered
much of North America, Europe and Asia. As temperatures rose,
the glaciers melted, retreating north. Animals that liked cool
climates walked, swam or flew to the new lands exposed by the
melting glaciers. Plants migrated by spreading their seeds. In the
warmer, drier south, old trees died. But in the cool, wet north,
their seedlings thrived. Over time, the forest continued to inch
northward, eventually reaching its current location,
and the boreal forest as we know it came to be.

Where Is the Boreal Forest?

The boreal forest is our planet's largest land-based biome. Also called taiga, the forest thrives in northern regions, forming a scarf around the neck of the world. Sixty percent of the forest is in Russia. Twenty-nine percent is in Canada. Other cold northern areas, like Alaska and Scandinavia, also have boreal forests.

There are many types of habitats in the biome. Diverse habitats provide homes for a diversity of species. There are birds in the trees and mammals in the bushes. There are fish and frogs in the rivers and the bogs. Some species stay all year. Others only visit.

Parts of the biome are so remote, few humans have ever seen them. But the boreal forest affects everyone. Its trees clean our air, and its wetlands clean our water. The biome also slows global climate change. It is a vast — and vital — wilderness.

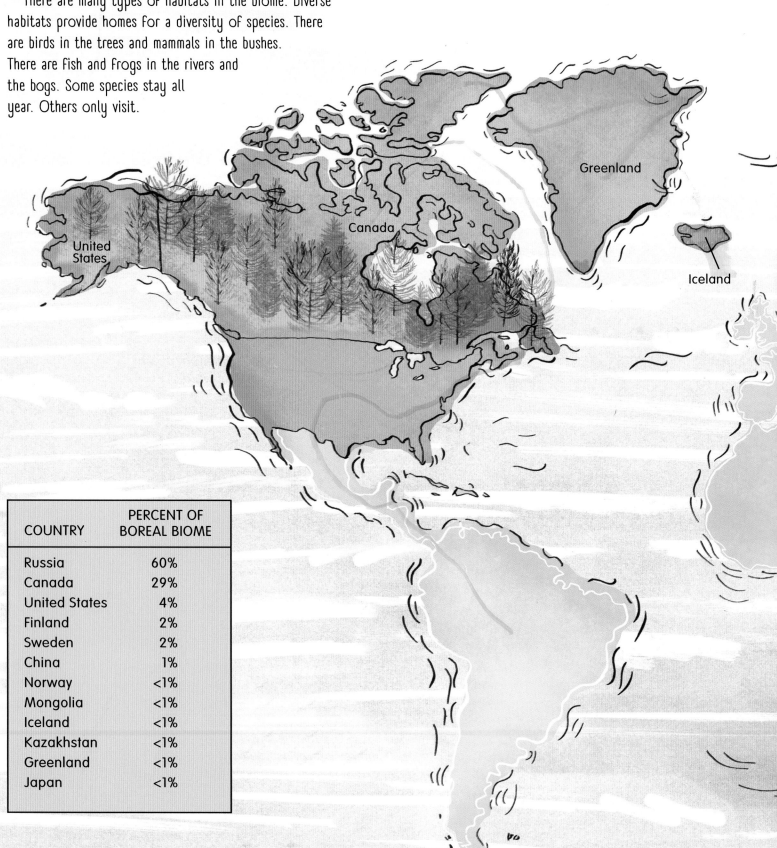

COUNTRY	PERCENT OF BOREAL BIOME
Russia	60%
Canada	29%
United States	4%
Finland	2%
Sweden	2%
China	1%
Norway	<1%
Mongolia	<1%
Iceland	<1%
Kazakhstan	<1%
Greenland	<1%
Japan	<1%

A Watery Wood

There's more fresh water in the boreal forest than anywhere else on Earth, with more than six hundred thousand lakes in Canada alone.

Sweden

Finland

Norway

Russia

Kazakhstan

Mongolia

China

Japan

RUSSIA

Winter

Snow falls from a flat, gray sky. It smothers a spruce tree, which creaks and cracks.

A flying squirrel peers out of a cavity in the trunk. Her breath forms tiny ice crystals in the air. They rustle on the snowy boughs, making a sound that Russians call "the whisper of the stars."

Snow blankets a nearby birch tree, still thick with tasty catkins. The squirrel charges along her branch and launches herself toward the meal. The spruce shivers and — *whoomp!* — snow drops to the forest floor.

Up in the Air

Siberian flying squirrels inhabit boreal forests from Finland to Japan. They almost never walk on land. Why would they? They can travel up to 50 m (164 ft.) in a single glide.

Boreal Trees

Deciduous trees such as birch, poplar and aspen are common in the southern boreal forest. Farther north, there are more conifers, such as spruce, pine and fir.

To prepare for winter, deciduous trees drop their broad leaves. In contrast, most conifers are "evergreen," keeping their needles year-round. Needles contain resins that help prevent freezing. Spruces and firs have another wintry adaptation: they are slim, cone-shaped trees with sloping branches. Heavy snow slides off instead of piling up, keeping the branches from breaking.

Winter's Chill

Winters in the boreal forest are long and terribly cold. In northern Europe and Asia, snow covers the ground up to ten months a year. Typical winter temperatures are between −20°C and −40°C (−4°F and −40°F). In 2013, temperatures in the forest village of Oymyakon, Russia, plunged to −71°C (−96°F). It was the lowest temperature officially recorded in the biome.

Snow Living

Once on the ground, snow changes. Exposed to cold air, the crust hardens and strengthens. Small animals can walk on it without falling through. Against the warmer soil, the bottom of the snowpack melts and refreezes. It becomes thin and fragile. Cracks form, creating highways for insects. Animals such as voles, shrews and mice can easily tunnel through the drift.

Like down blankets, layers of snow trap the body heat of living things. This extra warmth protects animals that might freeze to death on the snowy surface. To offer this protection, a snowbank must be at least 20 cm (8 in.) thick.

Small but Smart

Shrews are the boreal forest's smallest mammals. Weighing less than six paper clips, the Eurasian least shrew is smallest of all.

To save energy, some mammals hibernate in winter. Shrews use a different trick — they shrink! Their muscles, bones and organs (even their brains) shrink to about half their normal sizes. Smaller shrews need less energy from food to survive. That's good because, in winter, food, such as beetles, can be harder to find.

Beneath the trees, the snow settles over a bilberry bush. Its naked twigs are stuck in the drift, forming bridges to the warmer soil below. A beetle follows one down, seeking shelter from the cold.

The air is warmer in the space under the snow, just above freezing. It smells of old leaves and damp fur. A shrew scurries through frosty tunnels. The beetle darts and dodges, but cannot escape. *Crunch!* The hungry shrew continues his hunt. As he runs, his body heat melts the tunnel walls. They refreeze behind him, and delicate crystals, known as depth hoar, bloom in the darkness.

Snowdrifts glisten in a moonlit clearing. From its perch on a Scots pine, a boreal owl listens. As dawn breaks, she plunges, legs swinging forward. Snow explodes on impact, and the owl sinks below the surface. Struggling free, she flies back to the trees, a vole clutched in her talons.

Reindeer pass below the owl, moving into the shelter of the woods. Witch's hair lichen dangles from the branches above. Some deer raise their heads to taste. Others seek lichens growing on the ground. They grunt, pawing at the snow. The wind catches the loosened snowflakes and carries them away.

Winter Meals

Like other owls, boreal owls have one ear pointing up and one pointing down. Sounds reach each ear at slightly different times. This lets owls hear prey moving at different depths under the snow.

During blizzards, it's often too windy to fly. Owls store extra prey to eat on stormy nights. But boreal owls aren't strong enough to bite into frozen voles, mice or shrews. Instead, they sit on their snack until it thaws enough to eat!

NORWAY

Protecting the Herds

The Saami are an Indigenous people who live in Norway, Sweden, Finland and western Russia. For thousands of years, they have survived by herding reindeer. Reindeer provide food, furs and transportation. They are central to Saami culture.

Winters can be difficult for reindeer. When snow melts and then refreezes, a hard ice the Saami call bodneskárta may form on the ground. Reindeer can't break this ice to reach the lichens growing below. If they can't find other foods, such as tree-growing lichens, many reindeer starve.

Climate change has made these "lockouts" more common. That's why the Saami are combining their Traditional Knowledge of snow with satellite photos and weather-forecasting technology. They hope to predict which pastures will be open and which will be locked. This will help the Saami, and their reindeer, survive in a changing forest.

Wind stirs the snow that covers a frozen lake. Just below the ice, lake trout circle. Less than 5 percent of the morning sunlight penetrates the crust. The fish can barely see the shrimp and minnows they hunt.

With her poor eyesight, the star-nosed mole doesn't notice the gloom. Swimming along the lake bed, she blows a bubble. Breathing it back in, she scents her prey. The mole probes the mud with her star. She finds a leech and snatches it with tweezer-like front teeth. *Slurp!* Dinner is served. Belly full, the mole clambers into a tunnel in the bank, heading for her dry den.

Marvelous Moles

Star-nosed moles are named for the twenty-two tentacles that fan out around their noses, like the rays of a star. The star is only 1 cm (0.4 in.) across, but it contains over 100 000 touch receptors. That's five times more than a human hand!

While hunting, moles touch their stars to thirteen places per second. They can find, catch and eat a worm or insect in about a tenth of a second.

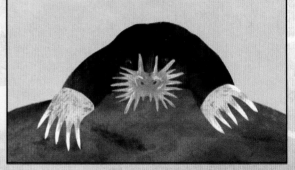

Frosty Fish

Fish are cold-blooded, meaning their body temperature matches the temperature of their environment. In winter, boreal lake water is between 0°C and 4°C (32°F and 39°F). Many fish find it difficult to swim at such low temperatures. They spend the winter resting, saving energy in a kind of hibernation. They begin hunting again in spring.

Some fish, like lake trout, prefer cold water. They spend all winter searching for prey. So do burbot, which are eel-shaped fish. In fact, burbot do most of their hunting in winter, when there is little competition from other fish. They hibernate during summer, instead.

Power Plants

Photosynthesis is a process that plants use to make food. First, their leaves inhale, absorbing carbon dioxide from the air. Inside the leaves, carbon dioxide combines with water and the sun's energy. This produces sugar, which gives plants the food energy they need to grow. Photosynthesis also produces oxygen, which plants exhale into the atmosphere.

The carbon dioxide that plants remove from the air ultimately becomes biomass — their living roots, stems and leaves. By capturing and transforming carbon dioxide, plants slow climate change. Worldwide, boreal forests capture about 8.3 trillion kg (18.3 trillion lb.) of carbon from the atmosphere each year. That's the weight of more than 50 million blue whales.

Thirsty Trees

In spring and summer, when the soil has thawed, plants absorb water through their roots. They use water for photosynthesis but also to cool themselves. In their leaves, liquid water absorbs heat and turns into vapor. As plants exhale the vapor, they also release the heat. Sweaty humans cool off in a similar way.

Movement of water from the soil through plants and into the atmosphere is called transpiration. One Norway spruce transpires up to 175 L (46 gal.) per day! Boreal transpiration is a major component of the global water cycle.

Spring

Near a different lake, high in the mountains, spring sun warms a stately fir. Perched in its branches, a sable yawns, basking in the light.

In the frozen soil, the tree's roots find only ice. But there's still a little moisture stored in its trunk. Water pumps from trunk to branch to twig to needle. The tree breathes in, waking from its winter slumber.

The sun is higher now — the fir is getting hot. The water that cools the tree is almost gone. If it can't drink soon, it will die of thirst.

But the days are getting longer, and the snow has begun to melt.

JAPAN

Down in the Dirt

Forest soil forms in layers. On top are fallen leaves and twigs, called leaf litter. Next is organic soil, containing humus (decomposing litter) mixed with clay, pebbles or sand. Deeper layers are made entirely of minerals that have broken off the underlying bedrock.

Some boreal soils also contain permafrost: soil or rock that's been frozen for at least two years. Most common in the northern boreal forest, permafrost lies under one-third of the biome worldwide. In Japan, permafrost can be up to 26 m (85 ft.) thick, about as deep as a seven-story building is tall.

In soils containing permafrost, only the upper, "active" layers thaw each spring. Deeper layers stay locked in ice. As climate warms, however, many active layers are getting deeper and moister. In some areas, boreal plants are dying because of these changes in their soils.

Up in the Mountains

Boreal forests grow in the mountains of Kazakhstan, Mongolia, northeast China and northern Japan. This is possible because mountaintops have cool climates: the temperature change from going 305 m (1000 ft.) up a mountain is about the same as traveling 400 km (248 mi.) north. Likewise, boreal forests typically grow only on the cooler north-facing slopes. Sunnier south-facing slopes are home to temperate forests instead.

On a tree-covered slope, water flows. It drips from icicles — *plink! plunk!* — and puddles on the snow below. Melting drifts crack and crumble. Water seeps through fallen leaves but cannot penetrate the still-frozen soil. It runs over the earth in sun-streaked ribbons, braiding together, pulling apart, draining into a mountain creek.

On the banks, ferns stretch and unfurl. After a long winter, a hungry raccoon dog emerges from his den. He splashes in the shallows and snuffles along the shore. Is that a newt he smells? He needs to bring back a catch. Pups are on their way, and his pregnant mate is hungry.

Small creeks become a bigger one, rushing north. Water surges over groaning ice. *Craaaack!* Chunks break free, bobbing downstream. They jam in the creek's elbow, blocking the flow. The creek bursts its banks, flooding the surrounding forest.

Safe above the soggy soil, flies buzz and mosquitoes hum. Birds swoop and peck to catch the insects, feasting after their long migration back to the biome. In a hollow poplar, endangered Chinese merganser chicks jostle at the lip of their nest. Their mother calls from the creek below, then dives for fly larvae while she waits. Gathering their courage, the ducklings leap, tumbling to the earth like downy raindrops. Together, they waddle to the water for their very first swim.

Sharing the Feast

Billions of migratory birds flock to the boreal forest each spring. They come for the insects — plentiful and nutritious food for hungry chicks. Birds share the abundance by hunting insects in different places: in trees and shrubs, on the ground and even in the air while flying.

The forest's bats also eat insects. While birds hunt mostly during the day, bats prefer to hunt at night. This gives everyone a chance to eat.

Bad Bugs

Boreal trees are tasty treats for insects, most of which are relatively harmless. But in some years, the populations of certain insect species increase in huge numbers. This is called an outbreak. An outbreak of gypsy moths will eat every leaf for miles, killing millions of trees. Trees that survive the moths are weakened and become targets for other pests, such as bark-eating beetles.

Cold winters kill insects, helping control outbreaks. But because of climate change, boreal winters are warming up. Pest insects are spreading farther north and may become a serious threat to the forest.

Creeks converge and merge, forming a sleepy river. The river flows past old pines, then cuts through a grove of young aspen and birch. It spills into a waterfall, sending ripples through the broad, still lake below.

A moose stands in the shallows. Stretching her neck, she nibbles the twigs and buds of the willows that line the shore. Her twin calves splash and play, stirring the rising mist with their spindly legs. In the distance, a loon yodels. *Kuik-kukuik-kukuik!* The moose lifts her head at the sound, nostrils flaring as she scents for danger. All is peaceful, so she takes another bite.

The Race For Space

Boreal trees can be killed by fire, insect outbreaks or strong winds that knock them down. These disturbances are both natural and important. They clear space where new trees can grow, and seedlings compete for this open space. Sun-loving deciduous trees, such as aspen and birch, grow faster than most conifers. They dominate young forests, forcing slower conifers to grow under their shade.

As the tall deciduous trees grow old and die, patches of light reach the longer-living spruce, pine and cedars below. These conifers can now grow tall and may replace deciduous trees completely. This change from one group of tree species to another is called succession.

Moose on the Loose

Moose prefer young forests that emerge after a fire. These animals start living in a burned forest while the tree stumps are still smoking! They know that soon there will be plenty of tender willow, aspen and birch shoots to eat.

A mother moose eats up to 19.5 kg (43 lb.) of leaves and twigs a day. This slows the trees' growth. It can even delay succession, preserving the moose's habitat.

RUSSIA

Sensing a Storm

The atmosphere's pressure starts to drop as early as three days before a storm. Some animals seem to sense this change in pressure. The early warning may give them time to prepare. Sparrows eat more so they won't be hungry while the winds are rough. Frogs may call for mates so that any eggs they lay will be moistened by the coming rain.

Scientists aren't sure how animals detect changes in pressure, but some think their ears are involved. The Vitali organ, found in the middle ear of birds, appears to respond to pressure changes. More research is needed, though, to figure out how the "storm sense" really works.

Making Rain

Of all the sun's energy that reaches Earth, half is absorbed by water. When the water gets hot enough, it evaporates, changing from liquid to vapor. Water vapor is very light. It floats high into the atmosphere, where it cools off and changes back to liquid. This change is called condensation. Condensation can also occur near the ground, producing fog.

In the clouds, liquid water droplets combine and grow, getting heavier. Eventually, gravity pulls them back to Earth as rain or snow. Scientists estimate that if all the water in the atmosphere fell at once, 25 mm (1 in.) of fresh rain would cover the entire surface of the earth.